HEINEMANN STATE STUDIES

Virginia
History

Karla Smith

Heinemann Library
Chicago, Illinois

© 2003 Heinemann Library
a division of Reed Elsevier Inc.
Chicago, Illinois

Customer Service 888-454-2279

Visit our website at www.heinemannlibrary.com

Designed by Heinemann Library
Page layout by Wilkinson Design
Printed and bound in the United States by Lake
Book Manufacturing, Inc.

07 06 05 04 03
10 9 8 7 6 5 4 3 2 1

**Library of Congress
Cataloging-in-Publication Data**

Smith, Karla, 1947-
    Virginia history / Karla Smith.
        p. cm. -- (Heinemann state studies)
    Summary: Provides a comprehensive look at
Virginia history,
  from the arrival of Europeans seeking riches five
hundred years
  ago to the 1990s, when the state became the
first to elect an
African American governor.
    Includes bibliographical references and index.
    ISBN 1-4034-0362-7 -- ISBN 1-4034-0584-0
(pbk.)
    1. Virginia--History--Juvenile literature.
[1. Virginia--History.]
  I. Title. II. Series.
  F226.3.S656 2003
  975.5--dc21

                                        2002153000

Acknowledgments

The author and publishers are grateful to the
following for permission to reproduce copyright
material:

Cover photograph by (main) The Granger
Collection, New York, (L-R) Bettman/Corbis,
Library of Congress, Bettmann/Corbis,
Bettmann/Corbis

Title page (L-R) The Marniner's Museum/Corbis,
North Wind Pictures, Bettmann/Corbis; contents
page Bettmann/Corbis p. 4 The British Museum;
p. 6 Chris Hellier/Corbis; pp. 7T, 10, 11, 15, 19,
24, 26, 27, 37 The Granger Collection, New York;
p. 7B The Marniner's Museum/Corbis; pp. 8, 9, 12,
13, 21, 22, 25, 30, 33, 36, 38, 39 Bettmann/
Corbis; p. 14 North Wind Pictures; p. 18 Steve
Solum; p. 20 Hulton-Deutsch Collection/Corbis;
pp. 29, 34, 42 Corbis; p. 35 Library of Congress;
p. 40 Naval Historical Foundation; p. 41 The
Marniner's Museum/Corbis

Photo research by Kathy Creech

Special thanks to Gary Barr for his expert advice
on the series.

Every effort has been made to contact copyright
holders of any material reproduced in this book.
Any omissions will be rectified in subsequent
printings if notice is given to the publisher.

Some words are shown in bold, **like this.**
You can find out what they mean by looking
in the glossary.

Contents

Early Virginia: Prehistory to 1700

Records show that Europeans explored the Chesapeake Bay in the 1500s. Soon after, Europeans began to establish colonies in the Virginia area. Before that happened, however, Virginia's First Americans—the American Indians—had been living on the land for thousands of years.

VIRGINIA'S FIRST AMERICANS: PRE-1500

The first people to live in what we now call Virginia were the American Indians. Based on their languages, there were three main groups of American Indians in Virginia: the Algonquian (Al–GON–key–an), Iroquoian (Ear–uh–KOY–an), and Souian (SOO–an).

Indian women gathered nuts, berries, and plants for food. They also farmed corn, squash, beans, and sunflowers. Men hunted animals such as deer, and fished for fish and crabs in the Chesapeake Bay and Virginia's rivers. The American Indians also used the rivers as highways, traveling in **dugout canoes.**

Virginia Indians built their houses using forest materials. They tied together small trees to make a frame, which they then covered with tree bark and mats

This drawing of an American Indian village in Virginia shows cornfields and pole-and-mat houses.

woven from swamp reeds. Their larger houses were called longhouses. Smaller, round houses were called wigwams.

The Indians made almost all of their clothing from animal skins and furs. They tattooed their bodies with a mixture of bloodroot and walnut dye. They used animal bones and shells to make jewelry, tools, weapons, and fishhooks.

SPANISH COLONIZATION: 1526–1571

Spain was the first nation to attempt to start colonies in what is now Virginia. In 1526, more than 600 Spaniards settled the Chesapeake Bay area. The colonists fought with the American Indians. Many colonists died from disease or starvation. The survivors gave up and returned to Spain.

In 1570, the Spanish established a settlement called Ajacán near present-day Yorktown. Eight Spanish Jesuits, led by a man named Father Segura, started the settlement. They were **missionaries.** At that time, the Spanish had colonized much of present-day Florida, and were interested in having more settlements to the north. However, the Native-American guide working with the Jesuits—along with other warriors from his tribe—attacked and killed the missionaries in 1571. The Spanish made no further attempts to settle a colony on the Chesapeake Bay.

ENGLISH COLONIZATION: 1584–1700

In 1584, Queen Elizabeth I of England gave Sir Walter Raleigh a charter to settle in

Don Luis

Sometime between 1559 and 1561, Spanish explorers kidnapped a Native-American boy from the Chesapeake Bay. The Spanish in Mexico gave him a European education and named him Don Luis. Don Luis returned to his homeland in 1570 as the Native-American guide for the Spanish missionaries of Ajacán.

the New World. A charter is a paper that grants an official permission. Raleigh sent explorers to look over the land.

John White and Thomas Hariot were two of these explorers. They lived with the Indians near Roanoke Island and even traveled north to the Chesapeake Bay. There, they met the Chesapeake Nation. White made drawings of the villages and Indian culture while Hariot recorded plants and animals. They took a good report back to Raleigh.

Sir Walter Raleigh was a favorite of Queen Elizabeth's. She made him a knight in 1585.

Raleigh sent a group of settlers to Roanoke Island in April 1585. It was too late in the year to plant crops. They suffered through storms and hot weather. When an English sea captain stopped to check on the settlers the following summer, they begged him to take them to England. Roanoke was not a good place to settle. The first attempt at a colony had failed. But Raleigh did not give up.

John White led more settlers to Virginia in 1587. They had wanted to sail north to the Chesapeake Bay, but the ship's captain left them on Roanoke. White sailed to England to get supplies. Three years passed before he returned in 1590.

White searched the island. The entire colony was missing. The only clue was the Native-American word *Croatan*, carved on a tree. Some believe

When the English first arrived, they did not know what to expect in the New World. Some thought they would find monsters, like those seen in this early map of the Virginia coast.

the colonists tried to move to Croatoan Island, home to the Croatan Indians. The ship's captain refused to search beyond Roanoke Island, so the ship returned to England without finding any colonists. The missing group of colonists became known as the "Lost Colony." The next group of English settlers did not arrive for twenty years.

JAMESTOWN: 1607

Queen Elizabeth I died in 1603 and James I was crowned king of England. In 1606, King James gave a group called the Virginia Company of London a charter to start a colony. This group wanted to earn money from natural **resources** found near the Chesapeake Bay. They hoped to find gold and other precious metals and stones.

In December 1606, Captain Christopher Newport set sail with 160 people. The English settlers included **nobles,** merchants, and workers. They were all men and boys.

In 1607, English colonists sailed to Virginia aboard three ships: the Susan Constant, *the* Godspeed, *and the* Discovery.

On April 26, 1607, they landed near the mouth of the Chesapeake Bay. Even though there were more than 150 Indian villages in the area at that time, the settlers claimed the land for England. They then sailed up a wide river near the mouth of the bay. They named it the James River, in honor of King James I of England.

The settlers chose a **peninsula** on the James River as their new home. Since it was surrounded on three sides by water and a **salt marsh,** it was easy to protect. It had forests and what the settlers thought was plenty of freshwater. The ships could be anchored in deep water near the shore. The settlers built a fort. In June 1607, Captain Newport took part of the group and a load of lumber to England to be sold there. Almost 100 people stayed to plant crops, cut lumber, search for gold, and explore. They had to worry about making money for the Virginia Company of London and about surviving in a new **environment** they knew little about. They had to build homes and grow or trade food with the Indians in order to stay alive.

At first, the colonists were able to make their new home livable. But then a severe **drought** occurred, and the

When the English settlers arrived at Jamestown in 1607, they had no idea what the future would hold.

local Indians did not have enough food to trade with colonists. Saltwater from the Atlantic Ocean and Chesapeake Bay flowed inland into rivers and streams, so freshwater was scarcer than they originally had thought. Disease spread through the shallow wells that the English had dug to reach freshwater.

In 1608, John Smith became the leader of the Jamestown colony because of his wilderness survival skills. He was also an excellent explorer, mapmaker, soldier, and trader. In August 1609, more than 200 additional settlers arrived in Jamestown. Now there were almost 300 people in the colony, but there was not enough food for the long Virginia winter.

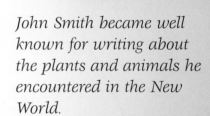

John Smith became well known for writing about the plants and animals he encountered in the New World.

John Smith decided that to survive, the settlers at Jamestown needed to split up. Some people moved to new settlements near friendly Indian tribes so that they could trade with them for food. In September 1609, John Smith was injured and returned to England. The remaining Jamestown settlers had problems trading with the Indians, who did not have enough food to spare. On December 24, 1609, a fire broke out and the fort burned down. Those who survived were so hungry that they had to eat rats and shoe leather. At the end of the winter, only about 60 of the original Jamestown colonists were still alive. That winter is known as the Starving Time.

In May 1610, another ship with new settlers arrived. But they found Jamestown in ruins and wanted to return to England. The ship's captain agreed, and they started back

Upon his arrival, Lord De La Warre became the governor of Virginia. He held that title until he returned to England in 1611.

down the James River. Before they reached the Atlantic Ocean, however, more ships from England met them. The Virginia Company of London had provided one of its representatives, Lord De La Warre, with ships, settlers, and, most importantly, supplies. The colony was saved.

The colony was expected to make money for the Virginia Company of London. The colony provided England with **raw materials** and natural **resources,** such as lumber and tar. In return, England sent manufactured goods, such as furniture and tools, which colonists could not make. Those goods were then sold in the colonies. In their first years at Jamestown, colonists relied heavily on food and products from England. But despite the lumber, pitch, and tar the colonists sent, they were not making enough money.

In 1612, John Rolfe, a settler in Jamestown, experimented with growing tobacco. He grew a type of tobacco that became very popular in

Colonial Goods

Jamestown settlers searched for ways to survive and make money for the Virginia Company. They found copper, which they may have traded with the American Indians. They also sent raw materials back to England to be sold for a profit.

Raw material:	Used to make:
lumber, pitch, tar	ships
iron	tools
lead	bullets
grapes	wine
silk worms	silk

The farming of tobacco became a way of life for almost all of Jamestown's early settlers.

England. Colonists soon grew tobacco everywhere. They sent barrels of tobacco to England in exchange for manufactured goods. Tobacco became the main **cash crop** for the Virginia Company. It was almost as good as the gold for which the colonists originally had searched. It ensured the success of the colony.

POCAHONTAS PEACE: 1614

However, trouble had been growing between the Indians and the settlers. As the settlers took more and more land to grow tobacco to send back to England, the Indians were forced from their homelands. The Indians fought back. They captured colonists and took guns and tools they found.

Chief Powhatan

Years before English settlers came to Jamestown, Powhatan was the chief of six tribes. By 1607, Powhatan had conquered 32 tribes between the Potomac and James Rivers. Powhatan ruled by force. He was so powerful that other tribes paid him a tax, or tribute. Tribes brought corn, deer, tobacco, and other goods to Powhatan in return for protection. When the English arrived in Virginia, Powhatan was the most powerful chief in the area. Powhatan's tribes fought the settlers many times. His power was slowly taken over by wave after wave of new settlers.

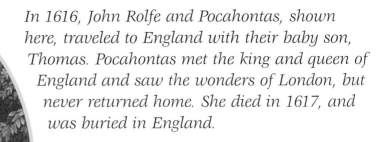

In 1616, John Rolfe and Pocahontas, shown here, traveled to England with their baby son, Thomas. Pocahontas met the king and queen of England and saw the wonders of London, but never returned home. She died in 1617, and was buried in England.

In 1613, an English captain named Samuel Argall kidnapped an Indian girl named Pocahontas and held her as a **hostage.** Pocahontas was the daughter of Chief Powhatan. Chief Powhatan was the leader of the Powhatan people, one of the largest groups of Algonquian speakers in Virginia at that time. Captain Argall wanted the Powhatan people to return the captured English colonists and weapons. Chief Powhatan refused, so Pocahontas was forced to stay in Jamestown. She was **baptized** a Christian and took the English name "Rebecca."

In 1614, Pocahontas married the Englishman John Rolfe. Powhatan promised not to fight the English as long as she lived. The fighting stopped, and this time period became known as the Pocahontas Peace.

1619: A Turning Point

By 1619, Jamestown was the capital of eleven settlements. There were 1,200 English settlers along the James River. Ten tons of tobacco had been shipped to England, providing a source of money for the colonists.

Three important events took place in Virginia in 1619. First, the Virginia Company of London sent 90 women to the colony. These women married the local settlers and started families, helping the colony to grow.

Second, each settlement elected **representatives** to the House of Burgesses, which was the first representative **legislature** in colonial America. The House of Burgesses met with Governor George Yeardley and a council to

make laws for the colony. That group was called the General Assembly of Virginia.

The third important event of 1619 was the arrival of a Dutch ship in Jamestown. The captain traded twenty African slaves he had on board for food. These first Africans were probably treated as **indentured servants.** Slavery was not made legal in Virginia until 1660.

Only white male property owners were permitted to vote for burgesses, representatives in the General Assembly.

THE MASSACRE OF 1622

As the colonists' settlements grew, the Indians became cut off from the forests, **marshes,** and rivers upon which they depended for survival. When Chief Powhatan died in 1618, his brother, Opechancanough, became chief of all Powhatan tribes. In 1622, Opechancanough plotted to end the English colony. He spread word to all the Powhatan tribes, asking them to kill the English settlers.

On May 22, 1622, Opechancanough and his warriors killed 347 English settlers. Jamestown had been warned in time by a friendly Indian to defend itself, but many other settlements were wiped out completely. In the next two years, 500 more settlers died of disease. By 1623, there were only a few hundred colonists left in Virginia.

THE END OF THE VIRGINIA COMPANY: 1624

Word of the murders and the sickness that followed reached England. Tobacco from Virginia was selling well there, but the Virginia Company of London was still losing money. Worried **investors** could no longer afford to send supplies to Jamestown.

Indentured Servants

Virginia had plenty of land, but not many people to work it. The Virginia Company needed more workers to farm and make goods in order to make more money. The company provided free transportation from England to Virginia for people who agreed to work when they arrived. After they worked a certain number of years, the people would be free to do as they liked. These people were called indentured servants. It was not an easy life, and indentured servants were sometimes not treated much better than slaves.

In 1624, King James I took the charter for Virginia away from the Virginia Company of London. He made Virginia a **royal colony.** Virginia's governors were now picked by the king. The royal governors, however, allowed the Virginia House of Burgesses to continue to meet.

Opechancanough, below, led his last uprising in 1644. He was captured and killed in Jamestown in 1646 by an English prison guard.

The king gave land in Virginia to his wealthy friends. More colonists came to Virginia, and **indentured servants** came there to work. New **plantations** and settlements pushed more American Indians out of their villages.

MORE CONFLICT WITH AMERICAN INDIANS

In 1644, Opechancanough ordered another attack on the colonists. His warriors killed 500 settlers. Volunteer **militias** from every settlement fought back against Opechancanough and his people.

In 1646, Opechancanough was captured and killed. The new chief signed a peace **treaty,** in which land north of the York River was promised

to the American Indians. The treaty did not last. It was the first of many treaties that would be broken by European settlers in America.

VIRGINIANS SETTLE THE PIEDMONT

By the 1670s, English colonists had filled the **Tidewater** lands with farms and plantations. Farmers began to move west into the **Piedmont** region. Colonists had not settled here before, because their boats could not sail that far west, past the **fall line.** But with more people, the rich lands of the Piedmont were now needed for new farms and plantations.

BACON'S REBELLION: 1676

Nathaniel Bacon was a Virginia farmer with land in the Piedmont. In 1675, Indians attacked workers on one of his plantations. Bacon asked the governor to send soldiers. The governor, Sir William Berkeley, refused because he did not want war with all the local tribes.

In 1676, Bacon led a group of men against the Indians of the Piedmont, killing both friendly and unfriendly American Indians. The governor sent soldiers to arrest Bacon, but he escaped.

Nathaniel Bacon, shown here burning Jamestown with his followers, was actually Governor Berkeley's cousin by marriage.

Bacon then marched on Jamestown with about 500 followers and burned down the **statehouse.** Governor Berkeley fled, and Bacon took over Virginia's government for two months.

The rebellion ended when Bacon suddenly became ill and died. Governor Berkeley returned to Jamestown and arrested and hanged many of Bacon's followers. King James I of England thought Governor Berkeley had been too cruel in this punishment, so he appointed a new governor. Order returned and Virginia continued to grow as more settlers arrived.

A NEW CAPITAL: 1699

The General Assembly of Virginia had been meeting in the statehouse in Jamestown. After the statehouse was burned down in 1698, the General Assembly decided to move the capital to Middle Plantation, Williamsburg, in 1699. This location was to the northeast, where more people were moving. The General Assembly met in the Wren Building of the College of William and Mary until they could build a new capitol building. The Assembly moved into the new building in Williamsburg in 1704.

Compare this map, which shows Virginia's English settlements in 1700, with the map on page 17, which shows settlements in 1775.

Settlement of Virginia, 1700

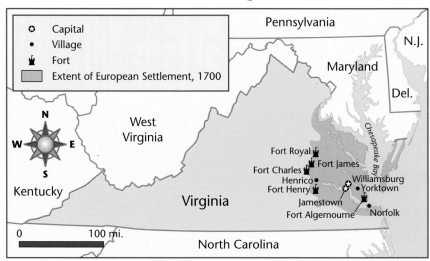

European Settlement: 1700–1763

By 1715, Virginia's population consisted of about 72,500 white settlers, 23,000 African slaves, and 1,000 Indians. Williamsburg was a busy city with a new capitol building and governor's house. The Virginia colony was still growing, and settlers continued to move farther west.

IMMIGRATION AND SETTLEMENT

More people from Europe **immigrated** to Virginia. German-Swiss workers came to work in the iron mines by the Rappahannock River. German **indentured servants**

By 1775, Virginia had been settled almost to the extent of its modern boundaries. This map shows the routes taken by different ethnic groups as they made their way through the colony.

Settlement of Virginia, 1775

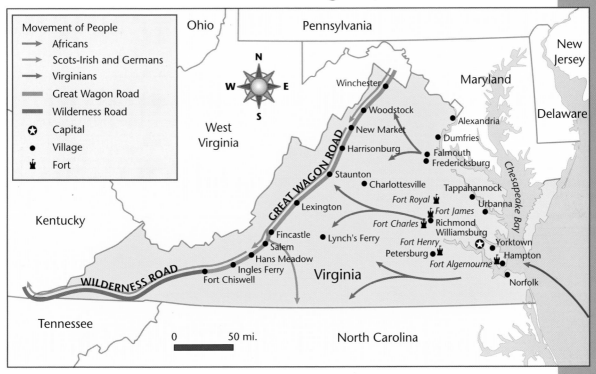

Movement of People
→ Africans
→ Scots-Irish and Germans
→ Virginians
— Great Wagon Road
— Wilderness Road
✪ Capital
● Village
♜ Fort

Ohio · Pennsylvania · New Jersey · Maryland · Delaware · West Virginia · Kentucky · Tennessee · North Carolina · Virginia

Winchester · Woodstock · New Market · Harrisonburg · Staunton · Lexington · Fincastle · Salem · Hans Meadow · Ingles Ferry · Fort Chiswell · Lynch's Ferry · Charlottesville · Fort Royal · Fort James · Fort Charles · Richmond · Williamsburg · Fort Henry · Petersburg · Fort Algernourne · Alexandria · Dumfries · Falmouth · Fredericksburg · Tappahannock · Urbanna · Yorktown · Hampton · Norfolk · Chesapeake Bay

GREAT WAGON ROAD · WILDERNESS ROAD

0 — 50 mi.

came to work in the mines and **blacksmith** shops. They called their settlement in the **Piedmont** region Germanna. French **Huguenots** also came to Virginia and started farms along the James River.

Governor Alexander Spotswood, then the royal governor of Virginia, wanted to explore new land. In 1716, Spotswood led a group westward. They climbed the Blue Ridge Mountains and then rode into the Shenandoah Valley. Spotswood claimed the land west of the Blue Ridge Mountains for the king of England.

The Blue Ridge Mountains made settling western Virginia a slow process until the development of the Great Wagon Road.

For more than 100 years, the Blue Ridge Mountains had made it difficult for settlers to move west. But in the 1730s, settlers found another way. They used the Great Warrior Path, a trail that had been used by American Indians for thousands of years. The trail, which later became known as the Great Wagon Road, is located in the valleys between the Blue Ridge and Allegheny Mountains. It runs from Pennsylvania in the north to Georgia in the south. Pioneers from the colony of Pennsylvania traveled down the road into Virginia and started farms in the Shenandoah Valley. Many of these new settlers were German and Scots-Irish.

THE FRENCH AND INDIAN WAR: 1754–1763

France and Great Britain both claimed land along Virginia's western **frontier.** The French mainly wanted to trade with the local Indians, and they built forts to protect the land they had claimed. The British, however, were interested in building towns in these same areas. As more settlers moved westward in Virginia, the governor needed land for new settlements. Since both the French and British claimed the same territory, conflicts arose.

In 1753, Virginia's governor sent George Washington, then an officer in the British Army, to ask the French to leave the land the British had claimed in Virginia. The French refused, and began asking their American Indian friends to attack English pioneer settlements. George Washington and his soldiers built Fort Necessity to protect the settlers. The French attacked the fort in 1754, and Washington was forced to surrender. The French and Indian War had begun.

Frontier Families

On the Virginia frontier, families were often miles away from their closest neighbors. Families lived in one-room cabins. Often, the only furniture they owned was one bed and one table. Everyone worked from sunrise to sunset to grow food. Men hunted animals for meat, and women made clothing by weaving, dyeing, and sewing cloth. Buckskin was made into hunting clothing. People often traded for goods they couldn't make. If a family had money, they used it to purchase salt, gunpowder, coffee, and store-bought clothing and shoes.

George Washington, shown here on horseback, was an aide to the British General Braddock during the French and Indian War.

19

The British king sent troops to drive the French and their Indian **allies** out of areas the British claimed as their own. George Washington, who later became the first president of the United States, led the troops of the Virginia **militia.**

Virginians participated in many important battles during the French and Indian War. In 1755, British troops led by General Braddock marched westward through the Virginia wilderness toward the French Fort Duquesne. The French and Indians hid in the woods and **ambushed** the British troops. The British were forced to retreat, and General Braddock died from a wound he received in the battle.

Key victories for the British in 1758 gave them an advantage. Great Britain gained control of the Atlantic Ocean. This meant troops in the colonies could receive supplies from Britain. It also meant they could keep French troops from receiving supplies sent from France. With no fresh troops or supplies, the French could not win.

The **Treaty** of Paris, signed on February 10, 1763, ended the French and Indian War. Great Britain gained control of nearly all of North America east of the Mississippi River. France lost all of its territory in that same area.

In 1755, General Braddock ordered his troops to march forward into battle without advance scouts. He was therefore unprepared for the ambush that forced him to retreat with his troops.

Revolutionary War Era: 1763–1825

Many Virginians were unhappy with King George III. They paid taxes to Great Britain, yet were not given much of a say about how they were ruled. Many colonists wanted to govern themselves, or to be treated as British subjects were treated in Great Britain.

TAXES AND THE STAMP ACT OF 1765

However, the French and Indian War had been expensive. King George III did not want to continue to pay British troops to protect colonists on the Virginia **frontier,** so he declared that no one could move west of the Blue Ridge Mountains. The king also decided that the colonists should pay for the war.

Parliament, the British law-making body, passed new laws to tax the colonists. But only people who lived in England had **representatives** in Parliament. Virginia colonists believed their own House of Burgesses should make Virginia's laws.

In 1765, Parliament passed the Stamp Act. The Stamp Act taxed printed materials such as newspapers and **deeds.** Colonists thought the taxes were unfair. Colonial leaders began writing to each other about what to do. These groups of leaders were called Committees of Correspondence.

Stamps such as these showed the tax to be paid on goods sold in the American colonies.

Before Patrick Henry, above, became a successful lawyer, he was a storekeeper and a farmer.

Patrick Henry, a lawyer in the House of Burgesses, spoke out against British taxes. Other colonists agreed with him. Their slogan became "no taxation without representation." They refused to buy British stamps or to pay the tax. Parliament **repealed** the law, but then put new taxes on glass, paint, and tea. Colonists then refused to buy those goods. Parliament repealed all taxes except the tax on tea.

On December 16, 1773, people in Boston, Massachusetts, dumped British tea into the **harbor** to protest the tea tax. Virginians read about the Boston Tea Party and decided to dump Virginia's British tea into the York River. In response to this, Virginia's royal governor shut down the House of Burgesses in May 1774. This left Virginia's colonists with no representation in their government at all.

FIRST CONTINENTAL CONGRESS: AUGUST 1, 1774

The Virginia House of Burgesses met secretly in Williamsburg on August 1, 1774, calling themselves the First Virginia Convention. They elected **delegates** to the First Continental Congress, which was to take place in Philadelphia, Pennsylvania. Peyton Randolph, one of Virginia's delegates, was chosen as president of the congress. The First Continental Congress sent a letter to King George III explaining why the British laws and taxes were unfair to colonists. The king refused to even read the letter and sent more British troops to the colonies to force the colonists to pay the taxes.

SECOND VIRGINIA CONVENTION: MARCH 23, 1775

The Second Virginia Convention met at St. John's Church in Richmond on March 23, 1775. Many Virginians did not want to fight against Great Britain. They were called **loyalists.** But then, Patrick Henry made a strong speech in support of colonial freedom from unfair British actions. He ended his speech with the famous words, "Give me liberty or give me death!" Virginia's leaders voted to give the Continental Army men and supplies to use against the British.

The First Continental Congress

Delegates to the Continental Congress met to protest the actions the British crown had been taking against American colonists. They talked about what they thought they should do to address those actions, and came up with a list of what they thought should be basic colonists' rights.

The delegates voted to stop trading with Great Britain until Parliament repealed its harsh taxes. They also decided to start preparing the colonists for a possible war.

THE REVOLUTIONARY WAR BEGINS: APRIL 19, 1775

In April 1775, British soldiers in Boston marched to Concord, Massachusetts, to take guns and ammunition away from colonists. Paul Revere rode through the night to warn people that "the British are coming." Colonists lined up to stop the British in the village of Lexington, and the first shots of the Revolutionary War (1775–1783) were fired!

SECOND CONTINENTAL CONGRESS: MAY 1775

The Second Continental Congress met in May 1775. Its members asked the Virginian George Washington to be the leader of the Continental Army. The colonies promised to send **militias** to support Washington.

THE FATHER OF OUR COUNTRY

George Washington knew that the British Army was much better trained and equipped than the colonists. However, he also knew the colonists had at least one advantage: they were fighting on their home ground. Washington knew it would be hard for the British to fight a lengthy war so far away from home. This was especially so because they were also fighting in other places in the world at the same time. Washington wisely led the Continental Army in several battles, either managing successful retreats or surprise victories. Without Washington, the war may have been lost. This is one of the reasons why George Washington is often called the Father of our Country.

This painting of George Washington shows the uniform he wore as a colonel in the Virginia Militia.

Virginians in the War

Other Virginians also helped in the fight against Great Britain. George Rogers Clark led soldiers through icy rivers in the Midwest in the winter of 1778, and won the **Northwest Territory** from the British. Virginia merchants and farmers gave the troops supplies. Women ran farms and businesses in Virginia while the men were away.

VIRGINIA BILL OF RIGHTS: JUNE 1776

In June 1776, Virginia's leaders met in Williamsburg. They elected a committee to write a bill of rights and a constitution. Virginia's constitution called for a general assembly elected by the people to make laws. The constitution also called for a governor of Virginia to be elected. Patrick Henry was elected Virginia's first governor in 1776.

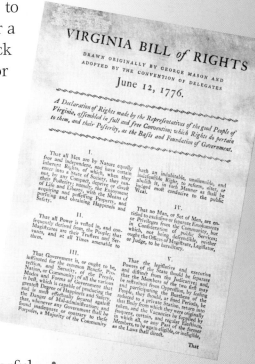

The Virginia Bill of Rights was largely written by George Mason. Mason was a wealthy Virginia farmer and friend and neighbor of George Washington. In the Bill of Rights, Mason introduced new ideas. He thought that the rights of individuals must be protected against the power of government and that the power of government should come from the people. Mason's list of rights were meant to make sure that a government could not become all-powerful and take away the rights of its citizens.

*The Virginia Bill of Rights was adopted by the **delegates** in Williamsburg on June 12, 1776.*

The Bill of Rights included in the United States Constitution of 1789 is based on the ideas of George Mason. One of Mason's ideas, which is found in the Constitution, says that all humans are created equal. Another says that freedom of the press and freedom of religion are important for a just society governed by and for the people.

DECLARATION OF INDEPENDENCE: JULY 4, 1776

News of Virginia's decision to support independence from Great Britain quickly reached Philadelphia. Other colonies soon followed Virginia's lead. **Delegates** were chosen from the Continental Congress to explain in writing the reasons the colonists sought independence from Great Britain.

Virginia resident Thomas Jefferson was the main author of the Declaration of Independence. It stated that the right to govern belongs to the people rather than to the king. It also said that all people are created equal and have the right to life, liberty, and the pursuit of happiness. It declared "the United Colonies free and independent states." Fifty-six people signed the Declaration of Independence on July 4, 1776. Seven of them were Virginians.

As a young student, Thomas Jefferson often spent fifteen hours a day studying. His studies helped prepare him to write the Declaration of Independence.

CAPITAL ON THE MOVE

Virginia's General Assembly felt it would be too easy for the British to attack Williamsburg, so they moved the capital to Richmond in 1779 in order to protect it. But in December 1780, the British marched on Richmond. The General Assembly then fled to Charlottesville. In June, the British tried to capture Virginia's leaders. A Virginia soldier, Jack Jouett, spotted the British near Louisa, Virginia. He knew that Governor Thomas Jefferson and other colonial leaders were in Charlottesville, so he rode all night in order to warn them. Most were able to escape.

SURRENDER AT YORKTOWN: 1781

In 1781, the British general Charles Cornwallis began a march to Virginia. He wanted to destroy enemy troops and cut off supplies to the Continental Army. He stopped to rest in Yorktown and waited there for British supply ships to arrive. George Washington was in New York when he heard about Cornwallis's position. Washington tricked the British into thinking he was still in New York while he actually marched his army to Yorktown.

In 1778, the French had agreed to help the colonists in their fight for independence. Now, the French general Lafayette brought soldiers to fight with Washington. The French Navy **blockaded** the entrance to the Chesapeake Bay. The trap was set. Cornwallis could not escape by land or sea.

Thousands of troops surrounded the British in Yorktown. For three weeks, they fired bombs and cannonballs into Yorktown. The French Navy defeated the British in a sea battle off the coast of Virginia. General Cornwallis finally surrendered the British army to Washington on October 19, 1781. In 1783, the **Treaty** of Paris was signed in Paris, France. That treaty officially ended the Revolutionary War. Virginia was a free and independent state.

The Americans could not have forced the surrender at Yorktown, seen here, without the help of more than 4,000 French troops, led by the Marquis de Lafayette and the Count de Rochambeau.

Religious Freedom

The following is taken from the Virginia Statute for Religious Freedom, written by Thomas Jefferson in 1786:

"Be it enacted [made law] by the General Assembly, That no man shall be compelled [forced] to frequent [attend] or support any religious worship, place, or ministry whatsoever, nor shall be enforced, restrained, molested [bothered], or burthened in his body or goods, nor shall otherwise suffer on account of his religious opinions or belief; but that all men shall be free to profess [state]... their opinion in matters of religion ..."

VIRGINIA STATUTE FOR RELIGIOUS FREEDOM: 1786

Before the Revolutionary War, the **Anglican Church** had received money and support from the British king. When the war ended, some people thought that the United States government should continue this policy. They thought that the government should tax all United States citizens and use the money to support recognized religions.

Thomas Jefferson and James Madison, however, strongly disagreed. They believed that the government should have no say in a person's religious beliefs, and that people should look only to themselves in matters of religion. The Virginia Statute for Religious Freedom, written by Jefferson in 1786, was adopted by the Virginia **legislature** with the help and support of Madison. It stated that people were free to worship as they pleased without interference from the government. The statute was later copied and included in the United States Constitution's Bill of Rights in 1789.

WRITING THE CONSTITUTION: 1787

After the Revolutionary War (1775–1783), the new states signed an agreement stating they would get along with one another. This agreement was called the Articles of Confederation. Each state had its own constitution and acted independently of other states, but problems soon arose. The states needed a better plan of government.

Delegates from each state went to Philadelphia. James Madison, George Mason, Edmund Randolph, and George Washington went as **representatives** from Virginia. Washington was elected to run the meeting, called the Constitutional Convention.

The delegates decided that the United States Congress, the lawmaking body, would be made up of two houses, or parts. Each state would send elected representatives to Congress. The ideas that George Mason and Thomas Jefferson had expressed in the Virginia Bill of Rights later became the first ten amendments to the United States Constitution. Those ten amendments are also called the Bill of Rights.

The new Constitution called for an elected president. George Washington was elected the first president in 1789. He served two four-year terms. Then he went to live at his home in Mount Vernon in 1797. George Washington had helped his country with great personal sacrifice. His friends said of Washington that he was "First in war, first in peace, and first in the hearts of his Countrymen."

FATHER OF THE CONSTITUTION

James Madison was a major contributor to the United States Constitution. He was responsible for the wording that guaranteed freedom of religion in the new country.

Madison also helped write the Federalist essays, which explained how the new government would work and why it would be best for the new country. These essays helped convince voters to **ratify** the Constitution. Because of his role in writing the new Constitution, James Madison is known as the Father of the Constitution.

LOUISIANA PURCHASE: 1803

Thomas Jefferson became our third president in 1800. He was the first president to live in the White House. In 1803, Jefferson bought the Louisiana Territory, which included the land between the Mississippi River and the Rocky Mountains, from France. The Louisiana Purchase cost $15 million, and it doubled the size of the country.

Jefferson wanted to know everything about this land. He hired two Virginians, Meriwether Lewis and William Clark, to explore the area for two years. They kept journals, drew maps, and collected plants, animals, and rock samples. A Shoshone Indian woman named Sacagawea helped guide them. In 1805, the expedition reached the Pacific Ocean and spent a cold and rainy winter there. The next year, Lewis and Clark reported back to Jefferson about the many natural **resources** they had seen.

When Lewis and Clark returned from their journey, they were each granted 1,600 acres of public land as a reward.

THE WAR OF 1812: 1812–1814

The Virginian James Madison became the fourth president of the United States in 1808.

Dolley Saves the Day!

Guns and canons boomed, and British soldiers marched closer and closer to the White House during the War of 1812. Dolley Madison would not leave until she saved her country's treasures. Her servants helped take down the painting of George Washington. Important government documents were packed into trunks. She hid the silver tea pitcher and sugar bowl in the well. Dolley and her helpers escaped just before the British soldiers arrived and burned the White House.

France and Great Britain were at war again, but Madison wanted to keep the United States out of the war. However, when British ships blocked **harbors** and attacked American ships in 1812, Madison asked Congress to declare war on Great Britain. The War of 1812 had begun.

British ships in the Chesapeake Bay tried to attack the cities of Norfolk and Portsmouth. When the attacks were unsuccessful, the British sailed to Hampton and destroyed it. The British also attacked and burned Washington, D.C., on August 25, 1814. Neither side really won the war, but the United States proved it was an independent nation that would not be bullied. On December 24, 1814, the **Treaty** of Ghent officially ended the War of 1812, although fighting continued into 1815. According to the treaty, all territory taken by either side during the war was to be returned.

THE ERA OF GOOD FEELING: 1817–1825

James Monroe, another Virginian, became the fifth president of the United States in 1817. In 1823, Monroe sent a message to Congress called the Monroe Doctrine, which said that other countries could not form new colonies in the Americas. While Monroe was president, the states of Maine and Missouri were added to the Union, and **canals** and roads were built or improved. A new road over the Blue Ridge Mountains helped Virginians move products east and west through the state. The years that Monroe was president are often known as the Era of Good Feeling, because the country was prosperous and growing.

Civil War and Reconstruction: 1850–1900

Differences between the North and South came to a head during the 1850s. These differences became larger problems and eventually led to a civil war that deeply affected Virginia. The North and South disagreed on three major issues: slavery, taxes, and **states' rights.**

REGIONAL DIFFERENCES

Virginia had depended on slavery for more than 100 years. **Plantations** growing **cash crops** such as tobacco and cotton needed slaves in order to make a profit. Northern states depended more on **industry.** They did not have many slaves, and did not approve of the plantation way of life.

People began to speak out against slavery. These people were called abolitionists, because they wanted to abolish, or do away with, slavery. Some helped slaves escape to the North. The route of hiding places from the South to the North was called the Underground Railroad. People who led the slaves out of the

Slave Revolts

Nat Turner was a slave in Southampton County, Virginia. In 1831, he led a **revolt** against slaveholders. He and his followers killed more than 50 people over two days. Turner and 52 others were brought to trial.

John Brown was an abolitionist who helped lead a slave revolt. In 1859, he led men to Harpers Ferry, where they took guns and ammunition that belonged to the army. After a bloody battle, Brown was arrested and tried for murder, treason, and inciting slaves to rebel. He was hanged. Many abolitionists considered John Brown a hero.

South were called "conductors." Abolitionists and the Underground Railroad further angered Southerners who felt that their way of life was threatened.

Northern and Southern states also disagreed on taxes. The North needed better roads and railroads to get its products to market. The South still sent most of its products to Europe on ships. The North wanted higher taxes to pay for better transportation. The South did not want to have to pay for roads and railroads in the North. Higher taxes on goods would hurt their trade with other countries.

The third main issue that the North and South disagreed on was states' rights. The South thought that individual states, and not Congress, should make laws about slavery and taxes. The South was therefore in favor of what it called "states' rights." The South said it would even leave the United States in order to keep these rights.

This Confederate flag was adopted by the South in May 1861. It shows only seven stars for seven states, but eleven states became part of the Confederacy.

THE NATION DIVIDES: 1861

In 1860, Abraham Lincoln was elected as our nation's sixteenth president. Lincoln believed that slavery should not expand into new territories. He also thought that states should not be allowed to leave the Union and start their own country. Just after he was elected, seven southern states—not including Virginia—**seceded** and became the Confederate States of America, or the Confederacy. The Northern states that remained part of the United States became known as the Union.

Brockenbrough House, in Richmond, became the headquarters of Jefferson Davis, president of the Confederacy.

On April 12, 1861, confederates took over Fort Sumter in Charleston, South Carolina. Lincoln asked 75,000 Union troops to take back the fort. Virginia, which had voted to remain in the Union eight days earlier, felt it could not fight against its friend, South Carolina. So, on April 17, 1861, Virginia voted to **secede** from the Union and join the Confederacy. By the end of May 1861, eleven states were part of the Confederacy. The confederate capital moved from Montgomery, Alabama, to Richmond, Virginia. On February 22, 1862, Jefferson Davis became president of the Confederacy.

CREATION OF WEST VIRGINIA: 1863

Not all Virginians wanted to secede. When the vote was taken in the Virginia General Assembly, all 55 votes from the western counties were against secession. After Virginia seceded, the western counties asked to stay in the Union. In 1863, the United States admitted them as the separate state of West Virginia.

ROBERT E. LEE

Robert E. Lee was a colonel in the army when trouble broke out between the North and South in 1861.

President Lincoln asked Lee to lead the Union army. Lee loved his country, but he was also very loyal to his home state of Virginia. Lee decided to go home to Virginia. He became the leader of the largest Confederate army.

BATTLE OF BULL RUN: JULY 1861

In July 1861, the Union army marched toward Richmond, Virginia. Confederate troops stopped them at Manassas. The battle—the first major land battle fought in Virginia—took place near a stream called Bull Run. Union soldiers were winning when Confederate general Thomas J. Jackson's troops arrived. Some Confederate troops began to fall back, but Jackson, a Virginia native, stood firm.

> *Almost half of all Civil War deaths— about 300,000—occurred in Virginia. This is because Virginia was so close to the Union-Confederate border.*

Major Civil War Battles in Virginia, 1861–1865

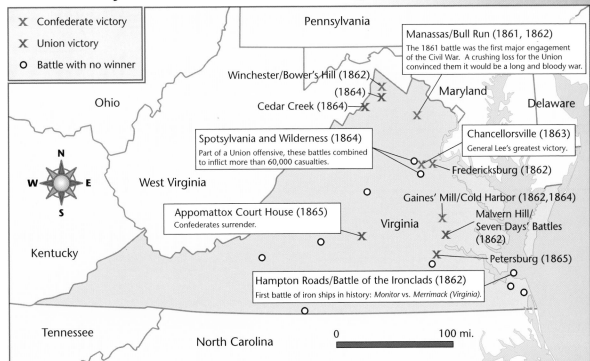

Pennsylvania

Manassas/Bull Run (1861, 1862)
The 1861 battle was the first major engagement of the Civil War. A crushing loss for the Union convinced them it would be a long and bloody war.

X Confederate victory
X Union victory
O Battle with no winner

Winchester/Bower's Hill (1862)
(1864)
Cedar Creek (1864)

Maryland

Ohio

Delaware

Chancellorsville (1863)
General Lee's greatest victory.

Spotsylvania and Wilderness (1864)
Part of a Union offensive, these battles combined to inflict more than 60,000 casualties.

Fredericksburg (1862)

West Virginia

Gaines' Mill/Cold Harbor (1862, 1864)

Appomattox Court House (1865)
Confederates surrender.

Virginia

Malvern Hill/
Seven Days' Battles
(1862)

Kentucky

Petersburg (1865)

Hampton Roads/Battle of the Ironclads (1862)
First battle of iron ships in history: *Monitor* vs. *Merrimack (Virginia)*.

Tennessee

North Carolina

0   100 mi.

John Ericsson, a Swedish-American inventor, designed the Monitor. *The* Monitor *fought the* Merrimack *at Hampton Roads in 1862.*

Confederate general Bernard Bee called out, "There he stands like a stone wall. Rally behind the Virginians!" The Confederates won the battle, and from that day on, General Jackson was known as "Stonewall" Jackson. The Confederate win at Manassas gave the South control of an important railroad junction. It was this battle that convinced President Lincoln that the Civil War would be neither quick nor cheap.

HAMPTON ROADS: MARCH 1862

On March 9, 1862, the *Virginia,* also called the *Merrimack,* was planning to destroy the Union's wooden **fleet** off Virginia's coast. The *Virginia* was a Confederate ironclad, or naval ship with iron sides. However, before it could attack, a Union ironclad called the *Monitor* arrived. The ironclads fought for four hours. The *Virginia* then sailed up the Elizabeth River to avoid getting stuck during low tide. Neither side won the battle.

FREDERICKSBURG: DECEMBER 1862

On December 12, 1862, Union soldiers led by General Ambrose Burnside crossed the Rappahannock River and drove the Confederates from Fredericksburg, Virginia. The goal of the Union was to capture Richmond, the Confederate capital. On December 13, the Union army marched out of Fredericksburg and met Confederate soldiers who were waiting on hills behind a stone wall. Union troops rushed forward, but not one made it past the

Black Civil War Soldiers

Abraham Lincoln's Emancipation Proclamation stated that all slaves living in the Confederate states would be free on January 1, 1863. The proclamation also allowed African Americans to join the Union army and navy, which contributed to the North's victory in the war. Thirty thousand Virginia slaves left their homes and joined Union forces.

hills or the wall. Nearly 5,600 Union troops had been killed or wounded by the end of the day. Richmond was saved, and the Union army withdrew.

SURRENDER AT APPOMATTOX: APRIL 1865

Lee kept the Union out of Richmond for four years. Then, Ulysses S. Grant was put in charge of the Union army. Grant cut off supplies to Richmond, and marched his troops into that city. Lee's army marched south, hoping to join with more Confederate troops in North Carolina. However, he was blocked by the Union army at Appomattox. Robert E. Lee knew then that he would have to surrender.

On April 9, 1865, Lee surrendered to Grant in the Virginia town of Appomattox Court House. General Grant allowed Confederate soldiers who owned horses to keep them. He also allowed officers to keep their weapons. A sad General Lee rode back to his headquarters. He told his men to go home, plant their crops, and obey the law. The war was over.

Virginia was in ruins. Cities and farms were burned. Bridges

Less than a month after Lee accepted Grant's terms of surrender, the rest of the Confederate army lay down its arms against the north.

Grant's army had captured Richmond six days before Lee surrendered. But the confederates had burned their own city so that the Union could not benefit from its factories or supplies. After the war ended, the citizens of Richmond returned to the city and found themselves with nothing.

and railroads were destroyed. Banks were closed, and Confederate money was useless. Freed slaves could not make a living. More than 15,000 people from Virginia had been killed in the war. Virginia had no working state government. Military leaders from the North were put in charge.

RECONSTRUCTION: 1865–1877

The period of time following the Civil War is known as Reconstruction. The Reconstruction Act of 1867 placed Virginia under army rule. This act also provided that Virginia draw up a new state constitution. A Virginia constitutional convention met in December 1867. Nearly one of every four members was African American. A constitution was adopted in 1869. It gave African Americans the right to vote and provided for a system of public schools. During Reconstruction, the Freedman's Bureau helped freed slaves get food, clothing, shelter, and jobs. More than 200 schools were set up to help former slaves learn new skills. The fact that African Americans could now vote meant that they started to have a political voice in Virginia. Virginia was readmitted to the Union on January 26, 1870.

SEGREGATION AND JIM CROW

African Americans gained many rights during Reconstruction. However, many whites were not happy to see their way of life changing. When Reconstruction ended in 1877 with the withdrawal of **federal** troops, African Americans faced **discrimination.** A tax was charged in order to register to vote, and only wealthy people could pay the tax.

This train station at Rosslyn, Virginia, demonstrates the Jim Crow laws in effect in post–Civil War Virginia. It shows two separate waiting rooms, one for whites and one for African Americans.

People had to pass a test in order to vote, and African Americans were usually asked more difficult questions in order to try to prevent them from voting. African Americans began to lose the rights they had so recently gained.

Cities and towns passed laws that segregated, or separated, African Americans and whites in public places, such as schools, restaurants, and theaters. These laws were called Jim Crow laws. Partly in response to these harsh laws, black churches began to spring up in nearly every Virginia town. The churches served as political, cultural, educational, and social centers for the black community.

END OF THE 1800s

As the 1800s drew to a close, Virginia was changing quickly. Virginia's cities had experienced growth during the Civil War, when many moved there to find jobs. The opening of new factories in the 1880s brought even more people to Virginia's cities to work.

The end of slavery meant the end of the **plantation** way of life in Virginia. **Industries** developed quickly. Tobacco and cotton were still important, but now there were cigarette factories and cotton textile plants that could produce more goods at a faster rate. New railroad lines and steam locomotives helped transport goods to and from Virginia's cities, as well as toward the coast, where they could be shipped overseas. By 1900, however, 85 percent of all Virginians still lived in small, rural areas.

Recent Virginia History: 1900 to Present

At the start of the 1900s, Virginians started to look out even more at the world around them. They were well on their way to becoming a part of the world at large.

WORLD WAR I: 1914–1918

In 1912, the Virginian Woodrow Wilson was elected 28th president of the United States. In 1914, World War I (1914–1918) began in Europe. President Wilson tried to keep the United States out of the war, but German U-boats, or submarines, began sinking American ships. The United States finally entered World War I in 1917. Norfolk, Virginia, became the navy training and supply center.

People came to Virginia from all over the United States to help build ships. Arlington and Alexandria, near the

This photograph from May 1917 shows submarine chasers, small boats able to destroy enemy submarines, being built at the Norfolk navy yard.

Pay As You Go

Virginia's governor Harry F. Byrd had a plan to help rebuild roads during the hard times of the Great Depression. He thought that a gasoline tax would make money to pay for highway construction. This plan was called "Pay as You Go." Soon other states began taxing gasoline to help pay for their roads.

nation's capital in Washington, D.C., became home to many government workers. World War I was the first major step in Virginia's transformation to an urban state, in which more people lived in cities than in the countryside.

THE GREAT DEPRESSION

The United States entered hard times in 1929 when the Great Depression began. During this time, thousands of Virginians lost all of their money. Many people left the cities and returned to farms. Others worked for the **federal** government or joined the military. President Franklin Roosevelt began programs to put Americans to work. In Virginia, the program called the Civilian Conservation Corps built state and national parks. It built Skyline Drive along the Blue Ridge Mountains.

WORLD WAR II: 1939–1945

In 1939, another European war started. President Franklin Roosevelt did not want to get involved. Then, on December 7, 1941, Japan attacked the U.S. Naval base at Pearl Harbor, Hawaii. The next day, the United States declared war on Japan and its **allies.** More than 50 military bases were located in Virginia during World War II. Thousands of people moved to the state to work in these bases. Ships were built in Hampton Roads. Many of the new workers were women who had never worked

The USS Yorktown *launched from the Newport News shipyard. It was later lost at sea during a World War II battle.*

Thousands of women worked in Virginia's factories during World War II. Many of them continued to work after the war ended in 1945.

outside the home. More than 300,000 men and women from Virginia joined the armed forces during the war, and more than 9,000 Virginians died before World War II ended in 1945.

After World War II, soldiers returned home to Virginia to start families and find work in the factories. When the soldiers came home, they discovered that the state had greatly changed. Cities had grown and were stretching into new communities at their edges called suburbs. Virginia had become a state with more factories and businesses. More families owned automobiles than ever before, and new roads and highways were needed. However, some ideas in Virginia were hard to change.

INTEGRATION AND CIVIL RIGHTS

In 1954, the United States Supreme Court made a decision about segregation, or the separation of African Americans and whites, in a court case called *Brown v. Board of Education.* That case said that the "separate but equal" plan for schools was not really equal. It also said that all schools must integrate, or accept both African-American and white students.

Many people in Virginia felt the Supreme Court should stay out of what they thought was state business. Virginia senator Harry F. Byrd Sr. led a movement called Massive Resistance. Supporters of the movement thought that Virginia should refuse to integrate the public schools. The governor of Virginia at that time, Thomas B. Stanley, said "I shall use every legal means at my command to continue segregated schools." Some school systems even closed down for several years to protest the order. Many children in Virginia could not get an education.

L. Douglas Wilder

On January 13, 1990, the first African-American governor of Virginia took the oath of office in Richmond. L. Douglas Wilder was the grandson of slaves. He was born and grew up in Richmond. He went to college and then joined the United States Army. He fought in the Korean War. When he came home he went to law school. L. Douglas Wilder spent many years in public office. When he was elected governor, he became the first African American elected governor of any state.

One of the reasons that World War II had been fought was to defend democratic values in Europe. Many of Virginia's African Americans, especially those who had contributed to the war, felt that the same issues needed to be addressed at home. Old laws limiting the rights of African Americans in Virginia needed to be changed. After years of struggle, Congress passed the Civil Rights Act of 1964 that made segregation illegal. School systems across Virginia began to accept students equally. Public transportation and businesses changed their rules to treat people equally.

INTO THE FUTURE

In the past 400 years, the population of Virginia has changed from rural to urban. Revolutions have been fought here, and new countries have been born. People have come to Virginia from nations all around world.

Today, Virginia's future is bright. The state's long and storied history provides a solid base from which Virginians will help to lead the United States into the future.

Map of Virginia

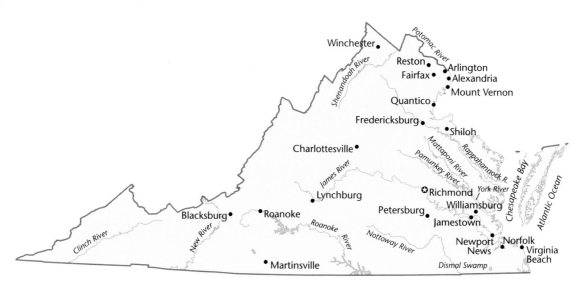

Winchester

Potomac River

Shenandoah River

Reston • Arlington
Fairfax • Alexandria
Mount Vernon

Quantico •

Fredericksburg •

Shiloh •

Charlottesville •

Mattaponi River
Rappahannock R.
Pamunkey River

Lynchburg •

James River

⊘ Richmond
York River

Williamsburg •

Chesapeake Bay

Blacksburg • • Roanoke

Petersburg •
Jamestown

New River

Roanoke River

Nottoway River

Atlantic Ocean

Clinch River

Newport News

Norfolk •
Virginia Beach

• Martinsville

Dismal Swamp

CANADA

ME
VT
NH
NY
MA
MI
PA
CT RI
IN
OH
NJ
MD
DE
WV
KY
Virginia
TN
NC
SC
AL GA
FL

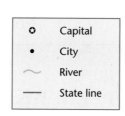

⊘	Capital
•	City
~	River
—	State line

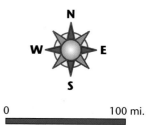

N
W E
S

0 ——————— 100 mi.

Timeline

1570	Spanish **missionaries** try to settle in Virginia along the York River.
1585	England sends John White to find a good place for "Virginia."
1590	Colonists disappear from Roanoke Island and become the "Lost Colony."
1607	Jamestown is settled.
1612	John Rolfe plants tobacco and Virginia planters have a **cash crop.**
1619	House of Burgesses established; first Africans brought to Virginia; first women arrive in the colony.
1622	American Indians kill one-third of Virginia's colonists.
1624	Virginia Company fails and Virginia becomes a **royal colony.**
1676	Nathaniel Bacon leads a **revolt** against Virginia's royal governor.
1754	French and Indian War begins.
1763	**Treaty** of Paris gives land east of the Mississippi River to Great Britain.
1765	Stamp Act leads to anger among colonists.
1776	Thomas Jefferson writes the Declaration of Independence.
1780	Richmond becomes capital of the colony of Virginia.
1781	Cornwallis surrenders British troops at Yorktown.
1787	United States Constitution is written.
1789	George Washington is elected president.
1800	Thomas Jefferson is elected third president of the United States.
1803	Lewis and Clark explore the Louisiana Territory.
1812	War of 1812 starts with Great Britain.
1831	Nat Turner leads revolt against slaveholders.
1859	John Brown raids Harpers Ferry.
1861	Civil War begins; Virginia **secedes** from the Union.
1865	General Lee surrenders at Appomattox Court House; slavery is abolished.
1870	End of Reconstruction; Virginia readmitted to the Union.
1917	United States enters World War I.
1941	United States enters World War II.
1954	Supreme Court orders integration of all schools. Harry F. Byrd orders Massive Resistance.
1964	Civil Rights Act bans **discrimination,** schools integrate.
1989	L. Douglas Wilder is elected as Virginia's first African-American governor.

Glossary

ally group or country working with another group or country

ambush to take by surprise

Anglican Church established church of England

baptize to admit into the Christian faith

blacksmith person who makes goods and tools out of iron

blockade to prevent someone from bringing in supplies

canal man-made river, used for transportation

cash crop crop that is grown to sell for money

deed signed document

delegate person who acts for someone else; a representative

discrimination prejudiced treatment

drought period of time with very little rain

dugout canoe canoe made by hollowing out the center of a tree trunk

environment what surrounds a settlement; the trees, water, air, and land

fall line imaginary line in Virginia dividing uplands from lowlands

federal related to the central government responsible for all states

fleet group of ships under a single command

frontier edge of unsettled area

harbor water next to land that is deep enough for ships to anchor, and that is protected from rough weather

hostage person kept for a promise of something

Huguenot person from a particular area of France

immigrate to move from one country to another

indentured servant person who agrees to work for a certain number of years in exchange for a free passage from one country to another

industry group of businesses

investor person who gives money to a business cause, hoping to earn more money back later

Iroquois Confederacy group of six Indian nations in the Eastern United States who came together and cooperated with one another

legislature group of people elected by their peers to make laws

loyalist person who remained loyal to Great Britain during the Revolutionary War

marsh area of wet land

militia arm;, in colonial times, the volunteer citizen army

missionary person who travels to other nations to spread his or her religion

Northwest Territory in 1787, an area of land that included present-day Ohio, Indiana, Illinois, Michigan, and Wisconsin

peninsula land that is surrounded on three sides by water

Piedmont in Virginia, the region between the coastal plains and mountains

plantation large farm in the south for growing crops like tobacco

ratify to formally approve

raw material natural material, such as coal, which is used to make other goods

repeal to take away or cancel a law

representative someone who acts in government for other people

resource material that can be made into something else to sell

revolt armed uprising

royal colony colony controlled and owned by a king or queen

secede to pull away from or to leave

statehouse building in which a state government meets

Tidewater region in eastern Virginia that sits on a low-lying plain

treaty agreement between nations or groups

More Books to Read

Barrett, Tracy. *Virginia.* Tarrytown, N.Y.: Marshall Cavendish Corporation, 1997.

Neshama, Rivvy. *Nat Turner and the Virginia Slave Revolt.* Eden Prairie, Minn.: The Child's World, 2000.

Thompson, Kathleen. *Virginia.* New York: Raintree Publishers, 1996.

Index

About the Author

Karla Smith grew up in a navy family and moved several times before settling down in Suffolk, Virginia. She has been teaching third, fourth, and fifth graders social studies since 1969. When she is not teaching, Smith enjoys exploring Virginia's waters in a sailboat.